WARRIOR

A STRONGER MINDSET

FIROZ TATA (WOLFY)

Contents

Preface

It gives me boundless bliss to bring my observations and experiences to the frontage by writing this book. I am confident that this publication will satisfy its purpose and will surely enhance the knowledge of its readers over the habits and techniques to lead a stronger, disciplined, content and warrior-like life.

This book is created by keeping in mind the stressful and demanding times we all are living in. Failures, stress, anxiety, sorrows, negativity, demotivation, rejections, dejections and expectations have become the dominant parts of our lives. They have drifted us away from inner peace and joy. Most of the time people feel disheartened, unfocussed and miserable, stopping them from paving their path towards determined and ambitious life.

'Warrior' is all about 'you' and 'us'. How you can change your outlook in order to endeavour ahead towards a strong mental frame. The book will guide its readers step by step through different approaches that will help to lead a better life. After several hours of brainstorming blended into various experiences, the chapters are designed in such a way that their reading, understanding and applications on self will set you towards a newer and brighter direction in life. After all, building a warrior mindset is all about practice and having the right shift at the right time.

This self-help book will assist in enhancing and augmenting the knowledge towards self in creating a better, calmer yet powerful and more productive version of you. I have no doubt that this book will be greeted and valued equally by all, especially by people who are mentally struggling in life for now.

Last but not least, 'Warrior' aims to inspire the readers to take the entire charge of their life in their hands and alter situations and surroundings accordingly for their progression. I have tried my level best to use easy to understand, reader-friendly and lucid language throughout the book. Let me assure you that this publication will not only go a very long way in increasing your mental strength and self-confidence, but will also assist you to discover a beautiful hidden version of self, cultivating a knack to pave the beautiful path of building a warrior within you.

It is highly recommended to read this book as a part of your evolution and a journey to become the best version of yourself. Importantly, the book has its deserved place on every warrior's reading list.

- The Author

Acknowledgements

I share my word of acknowledgement and heartfelt gratitude to my beloved mother Ms. Heera Minoo Tata. As a son, I express my earnest care and love to her. She has always been my strongest supporter no matter what. Each time she has raised my spirit and unconditionally encouraged me during my highs and lows in my several writing journeys.

I also extend my sincere acknowledgement to Notion Press publishers for providing a platform of Xpress Publishing through which my 24th book is published for sales in India as well as overseas.

Finally and importantly, I also want to thank every single one of you who has stuck with me since the last 15 years of my writing journey.

- The Author

CHAPTER ONE

Introductory Words

Most of the time many of us have felt that life is too hard to handle. Sometimes it seems like a grave struggle to get up each morning and do a long list of tedious things that we are expected to do. Many among us wake up feeling constantly tired, anxious and stressed. Life just seems to be giving too much toil on us. However, on the other hand, think about a soldier protecting his countrymen with a bulletproof mentality. He spends several rough nights with less or no sleep, unaware of when to see the family again, unsure whether or not he will survive or perish under an abrupt attack. He wakes up earlier than most of us, no time for a shower or a nice hot breakfast. Without a second thought leaps straight into action. He ignores his wounds, pains, combats against the enemies and even witnesses the painful scenes of his fellow soldiers shot dead or blasted by the enemies in front of his eyes.

A warrior mindset actually has nothing to do with guns, bombs and warfare. Today, as an eye opener, I got it. You are surely very exhausted because for five or maximum six days a week you have to work until six, seven or eight in the evening. Perhaps you do not even have a few quiet minutes to eat or a few peaceful seconds to drink water. Correct, your life is over and above stressed and too busy.

Actually, our lives are not really that hard as we imagine and like to portray to every other person. There are thousands and thousands of people out there with much worse living conditions than us. There are people who live with a crippling ailment and daily undergo several struggles for their basic survival. Many of them do this with smiles, dignity, grace and utmost courage in their hearts. This should put our heads to rest with shame. In fact, the lawbreakers or so called macho men that start fights on the roads and think that they are untouchable and tough are far from the reality of being a fighter.

Ask anyone who has seen or been into actual combat if they would want to fall in a deadly trap and risk their health and lives. This is about adopting a tough approach and not letting little things get you down. It is about pushing ahead with what you know is right and carrying accountability and adversity on your shoulders with poise and pride. It is about not letting your emotions get the better of you and not taking the easy way out to solve the problems. The point is that some people manage to stay cool and calm as a cucumber in even the worst situations and constantly thrive ahead. They do not allow small inconveniences or a lack of comforts to stand in their way. Such are the real heroes who put us to shame and make our grievances seem very petty indeed.

Instead of getting weary, hopeless, unfocussed and tempted by negatives, we must keep moving forward with a persevering and unstoppable approach. Our rivals should realise that there is nothing they can do to stop us achieving our goals. As career obstacles, relationship goals and financial plans can all crumble beneath our weak will and bad decision making ability, one should think of themselves as extremely proficient, strong minded and full of pride.

Self-discipline, determination and self-sufficiency are what will make us strong and will help to get what we desire. We will be unstoppable towards our achievements and will be able to live with ourselves and earn admiration from others.

However, developing a warrior-like mind is complex and challenging because it includes a number of different strategies and activities. In order for it to be fruitful, we need to possess a good intellect, how it works and how we can best adapt it to work for a specific situation. A question arises from where such a strong approach appears and what is the notion behind such a mindset? Of course, it comes from our image of the warrior and from their historical stories. It comes from tales of the bravest men and women who fought actual battles while staying focused, cool headed and sacrificed themselves for others while doing incredible things. However, for every heroic person who pushed themselves in the line of fire, there existed hundreds and thousands of people who kept themselves available for the sacrifices. Glamorizing warfare is in fact an awful idea as it is a truly dreadful state of affairs and very few people feel like warriors when they face the enemy.

Visualise if you had the mental strength to lie down in a glass box with hundred cockroaches for an hour or visualise if you had faced many life threatening medical situations. Compare such challenges against the absolutely minor tests that most of us undergo on a day-to-day basis. Hence, having a warrior's mindset and going through modern life is like lifting weights to bulge the muscles. Developing such a mindset is like a wholesome workout for our brain as well as for our overall views.

CHAPTER TWO

A Warrior Mind Through Examples

Self-discipline, courage, protectiveness, righteousness, resilient will, modest though, humble approach, growth-oriented, self-sufficient, confidence, caring nature, self-sacrificing, peaceful, focused, responsible, motivational, charismatic, noble and influential are some of the significant traits that a true warrior should strive for. These are some of the important attributes a person should look for to cultivate within him/her.

A warrior spirit includes being silent and calm on the outside, but possessing great intent, purpose and strength on the inside. A person holding such an outlook is not driven by impulse, but by better purpose. They neither bend to the will of others, nor give up when the going gets tough. We do not live on the battlefield and hopefully will never need to see combat, but there are plenty of ways and opportunities to demonstrate in which the warrior mindset will apply in our day-to-day life. Perhaps the easiest way to consider this is to look at all those times that we were not a fighter and we kept on quitting. These were the crucial times when our fear, anger or lack of motivation and resolve got the better of us.

- **Consider these six following examples:**

(a) Your boss needs you to complete an assignment before leaving the office. As you are exhausted, initially you bear a grudge towards the idea of staying late, but soon are compelled to work. Unfortunately, you rush through the work with less effort.

(b) Although you are unhappy in your relationship or job, you stay in it because you do not have the courage to tell the person. Moreover, you are too afraid of what the future might hold.

(c) You are working very hard to lose weight, but as you are low on energy you eat a large piece of pastry kept in the fridge or order some junk food from outside.

(d) You wake up in the morning and realize that your favourite white shirt is torn. You spend the rest of the day unnecessarily fuming on everyone, grumbling and not focussing on your work. This tiny problem has ruined your ability to stay focused and productive. It has also made other people feel bad for your behaviour.

(e) You get into a physical disagreement with someone in the street and hide or run away leaving your family and friends to deal with the situation on their own.

(f) Rain has forced you to call off your plans to visit a friend who was eagerly looking forward to meet you.

Although all these examples seem very different from one another, they essentially come from the same thing which is the mental weakness of an individual. Such weakness is often the source of our problems and landing ourselves into the things we know are wrong, or making excuses and avoiding goals.

- **Taking these six examples under consideration, let us look at how someone possessing strong mental approach might have advanced in the same situations:**

(a) Although your boss needs you to complete an assignment before you leave for home and you dislike the idea of staying late, nonetheless you complete the work to the best of your ability. Later you calmly request your boss to not put you in the similar position again.

(b) You are unhappy in your relationship or job so you discuss that unhappiness with the other person and look for the solutions to improve the situation. That might mean finding a new job or ending the relationship. However, it is better than dragging it out.

(c) You are trying to lose weight, but feel low on energy. Instead of having a large piece of pastry kept in the fridge or ordering junk food from outside, you decide to eat an apple. Soon you dig deep, find that motivation within and head to the gym.

(d) If you shrug and wear something else instead of white shirt, recognizing that this is a very small issue to pay attention to, give energy and time.

(e) After entering into a physical altercation with someone in the street, a person possessing a strong mental approach will make sure his family and friends are safe. A person tries to calm the situation as best as he/she can.

(f) It is raining out and you do not feel like going out, but still you know it is the right thing to do. You man up, get ready and you go.

Mentally strong people have healthy habits and they manage their emotions, thoughts and behaviours in ways that set them up for success in life. They do not sit around feeling dejected about their circumstances or how others have treated them. Instead, they take responsibility for their role in life and understand that life is not always easy or fair. They appreciate and celebrate other people's success. They do not grow insecure, jealous or feel cheated when others surpass them. Instead, they recognize that success comes with hard work, and they are willing to work hard for their own chance at success.

People having such a strong mentality and willpower stick to their code of ethics and work very hard toward their vision and beliefs for a better and prosperous future. They take new challenges as a learning experience and avoid doing things that make them feel good within their comfort zone. This leads to greater pleasure, peace and pride. Such an approach not only affects them, but also affects others around them. They do not feel entitled to things in life as they were not born with a mentality that others would take care of them or that the world must give them something without earning. Instead, they look for every single opportunity based on their own merit.

CHAPTER THREE

Our Goals and Code of Ethics

Certain important questions arise that how do we gain determination and how do we develop the unstoppable knack to never give up? It starts by knowing what we want to achieve and by creating a set of our own principles to follow. If we do not try to stand for something we believe in, we will fall for everything and anything. Moreover, if a person has no specific goal and set of values, then how is he/she expected to attach firmly to those values?

If we have not defined who we are and what is important to us, then of course it will be easy to get attracted towards effortless options like eating ready to eat unhealthy foods, watching meaningless television shows and movies for hours, wasting time on long hours of sleep, etc. It will be easy for us to be persuaded by the influence and the strategies of others. However, having a goal is what will give us the motivation and the energy to get up and work toward the things we truly believe in and are excited about to happen in life.

Think about some great world personalities like Arnold Schwarzenegger an Austrian-American actor, former bodybuilder, film producer, businessman and politician who served as the 38th Governor of California between 2003 and 2011 or Dwayne Johnson (the Rock) a former American professional wrestler, actor, producer and businessman. They are the living legends who have accomplished incredible things undoubtedly through their seemingly endless energy and their ability to get up every single day and know what they want to do in their lives. Can you imagine seeing the Rock look tired and dejected? Have you ever seen Arnold look frustrated and fed up? Such people have untiring vigour that arises from a farsighted vision and a goal. This is with almost all the successful people throughout history.

Once Arnold said, "*With my desire and drive, I definitely wasn't normal. Normal people can be happy with a regular life. I was different. I felt there was more to life than plodding through a normal existence. I have always been impressed by stories of greatness and power. I wanted to do something special, to be recognized as the best. I saw bodybuilding as the vehicle that would take me to the top, putting all my energy into it.*" The point is: knowing what we want from life will fuel us with energy, whether that is wanting the best for our family, achieving creative triumphs, to reach a certain point in career, etc.

Think about new parents. They have apparently endless energy and a will to sacrifice their sleep, finances, freedom and happiness to protect and look after their child. They can almost attain anything because they have found something precious and greater than themselves. A parent's unconditional love will give them a mindset of a warrior. However, one cannot rely on just that. In order to achieve the most and to build the best world around, we also need something that is essentially stirring us. In other words, we need a purpose and a goal to thrive that does not depend on anyone else. When we feel unwanted or unloved, we still should collect the strength to pull ourselves out of bed and do what is best for us, refusing to be distracted by unhelpful mentalities and desires.

Once we have our goal, we can find a passion, and once we have found a passion to pursue we will discover that we have endless energy and drive. We start to speak with more conviction and greater charisma. We gesticulate more when we speak about something close to our heart and that we are zealous about. This is because we are speaking portraying our body language that is corresponding with what we are saying. When people see us speak in that way, they actually see us as more alluring, inspiring and as a dedicated leader. When we actually believe in what we are saying, we will be more efficient at getting others convinced and believe in us. This will make us far more attractive and magnetic.

With our goals and objectives, we will better be able to make decisions and avoid needless interruptions. We will be more decisive and impressive. This is because we can consider every decision after questioning if this helps us to achieve our goals. If the answer is no, then we will try to do something else.

(1) Goals: The point of the goal is to have something that is greater than ourself and rather worth fighting for to achieve. This single-mindedness is something that was the dominant psychology of all of history's greatest warriors, although it took a very different form. Historically, we had samurai and knights. A samurai's training went to great measures to ensure their loyalty to a 'shogun' who was a master samurai. They would stay ready to lay their lives for their shogun, just as a king's knight would be willing to die for him and for the countrymen. Today though, this is dangerous thinking as we all are aware that most of the leaders are flawed and we have seen how blindly following them or a set of beliefs can lead to terrible outcomes including brutalities and atrocities. Hence, what we need to do instead is to create our own set of values and ideologies, rules to live by and a goal or a vision to strive for. We must never let others force us to act against our set rules.

Unfortunately, there is no accurately correct way to approach life. We do not know what is waiting for us on the other side of the corner to show us the actual meaning of life. It is up to each one of us to make our way by assessing standards, philosophies and rules to live by.

(2) Discovering our goal: Let us start with finding a goal greater than ourselves. It helps in striving forward with an intent. A drive that will be an important instrument in accomplishing. This might mean that we are set about to change the world for the better. Perhaps we want to put an end to hunger in the world, help slow down global warming, or perhaps we are interested in becoming a writer or a musician. Maybe we just want to accumulate wealth and get rich. However, no good goal is wrong. It is simply having a goal and something to be highly passionate about that will give us the fuel and the desire to keep going no matter what.

As goals are born from one's vision, we must visualize the way we want our lives to be a few years later. Imagine where we could be, what our surroundings would be, with whom we would be and what we may have accomplished. This should be a vision that will make us excited and energized. For inspiration, consider the times in life we were happiest, consider what we wanted to be as a child and remember some of our role models and what we have possibly learned from them. This will drive ourself toward a healthier change and greatness. It will get us out of bed in the morning to gradually structure and follow our goals. Hence, smaller and more measurable steps will help us to reach that point.

(3) Creating our own code of ethics: Surely this does not have to be our conventional set of rules. Ethics are born from what makes us happy while working on things that we love. Improving ourselves and protecting the ones we care the utmost makes us happier. Looking after our families, friends and loved ones, pursuing our passions, desires and working on self-betterment further contributes to society in a positive manner.

Whatever we believe our code to be, we follow them and then commit ourselves towards it. That way, we will not be pressured and persuaded by others and we will be able to fight for our values. People will know where they stand with us. Moreover, we should not be afraid to evolve and adapt our ideas over time. Thus, it is very important to keep reading and learning new things. Keeping up to date with things that interest us the most and awareness of the important events occurring around the world further helps. There is no worth in sticking to one set of goals or principles for an indefinite period and refusing to change them. Eventually this turns into a lie as much as any other.

A person should not be terrified to reconsider the way that he/she feels about certain aspects of the code. The point is that we will not break our code of conduct while it exists. We have standards to uphold and the simple act of upholding them will make us stronger, fearless and more imposing individuals. In the ideal situation, there should be some interaction between what we personally believe, our personal code of ethics and our goals. We must have a vision for what we think and what life should be like. Our goals are there to help us attain that vision, while our code of ethics guarantees that we do not fail to understand or appreciate a large situation, issue, etc., by considering only a few parts of it. Finally, all this results in us becoming a person who knows what we believe and know. Once we identify that, we will be an improved and more efficient individual in general.

CHAPTER FOUR

Fear, Stoic Philosophy and Death

When we think of a typical kind of a warrior, we will certainly visualize someone that is courageous, physically strong and apparently fearless. This is the kind of person that will walk into the line of fire, will voice out against injustice, take on enemies and slay their monsters that are much stronger. Although in our day-to-day lives, there are no real dragons and monsters to slay, they take on many other forms, such as illness, work pressure, conflicts, debt or simply the struggle of going to the gym every day.

(1) How to use fear setting: If you are a fan of reading self-help books then chances are that at some point or the other you may have secretly written down your goals. This is something that almost every expert seems to advise, claiming that it will help in accomplishing the dreams by better defining and visualising them.

What actually is fear setting? The general idea behind fear setting is that we are outlining the fears that are holding us back so that we can face them. In most cases it is assumed that after doing this one finds that fears are relatively unfounded. This helps to move forward and past them. Normally our fears are of irreversible negative outcomes. Thus, what we do is to write down the absolute worst possible outcomes for doing whatever we want to do, and then write down all the ways we would cope with the situation or possibly reverse it. Let us take changing careers as an example. This is something that a lot of people want to do, but feel held back by fear of the potential consequences. By defining those fears, one can minimise their effectiveness.

- **If you were going to write down some of the worst possible outcomes for changing career, it might well look something like this:**

(a) I might leave my job only to fail to find another job.

(b) This could upset my partner so much that he/she may leave me.

(c) I might get the job I want and find out I hate it more than my last job.

(d) I might apply to other jobs only to get rejected by everyone and end up hurting my ego.

- **Although these are all real concerns, we can think about the following ways to manage risk and reduce the impacts of those negative outcomes to find our fears almost vanishing:**

(a) Without informing anyone, I can look for a new job continuing my current job. This will avoid the risk of unemployment.

(b) If my partner leaves me in search of his/her comfort and happiness then I need to reassess that relationship.

(c) If I do not like the job I will find another and then I will feel more confident about job searching again in future.

Alternatively, I can discuss it with my boss and see if there are other positions available within the organisation.

(d) If I struggle to get accepted anywhere, I can work on my interview technique or improve my Curriculum Vitae (CV) or seek vocational guidance. All of which will be useful experiences anyway.

As we can see, the very worst scenario is probably not as bad as it appears. It may just mean living out of savings for a while or taking a small step backward in order to take two steps forward. Similarly, as there are various ways to minimise the risk of things going wrong, it is actually quite unlikely we will end up in those positions anyway.

(2) Stoicism and the warrior mindset: Stoicism is a school of Hellenistic philosophy founded by Zeno of Citium in Athens in the early 3rd century BC. Stoicism teaches the development of self-control and strength as a means of overcoming destructive emotions. The philosophy holds that becoming a clear and impartial thinker allows one to understand the universal reason. Its principles were founded and practiced by historical characters such as Seneca (a Roman Stoic philosopher, statesman and dramatist), Marcus Aurelius (a Roman emperor and a Stoic philosopher) and Epictetus (a Greek Stoic philosopher). Thus, Stoicism was an early approach to a warrior mindset. It was all about mental hardiness and about learning to expect and then live with things going wrong. In fact, many of us describe someone who is brave and courageous as being stoic. The Stoics believed that one's wealth, status, power, possessions and stature are neither good nor bad. They have no social significance with respect to the relationships with each other as all are equal. They held an opinion that external differences like ranks and wealth had no position in social relationships.

(3) The power of pessimism: If we tell someone that we do not think that certain things are going to work out as we expect, then they will often tell us that we need to step out of negativity and be more optimistic. Emphasising the positives and eliminating the negatives is the best thing one can do. Thus, being positive is a good thing and being anything other than that is unacceptable. However, is this really the best way for us to approach our problems? Or is it perhaps actually quite damaging to constantly be blinded by optimism? Does it leave us defenceless against disappointment? Is expected life to be constantly sunshine and flowers without thorns, the exact opposite of a warrior mindset? Wouldn't a warrior accept and embrace the fact that life will also be hard and one needs to toughen themselves up to deal with it? That is the view held by Stoics when we study their philosophy.

(4) The central philosophies of Stoicism: The general gist of Stoicism is not to try and shunt out negativity and pretend that bad things never happen. Rather one should embrace it and use negatives as a tool to excel. According to the Stoics, hope is the enemy because it means we are unprepared for the undesirable things. Thus, we are likely to be disappointed in the coming future. Instead, Stoicism advocates the notion of determined realism of recognizing the negative aspects of life and accepting the fact that many events occurring in our lives are out of control and are probably not going to be very pleasant.

(5) Using Stoicism in life: This might not sound like a particularly helpful attitude to take on things, but then that is because most of us are taught only to accept positive viewpoints. This is the general theme of countless self-help books and some movies in general. Dream big and you can get what you want! In fact, it is pretty much the driving force behind fame and success in life. However, the Stoics take the opposite approach. They prepare for the storm and learn to enjoy life even when things are not going that well. They recognize hardship as a challenge and an opportunity for growth and development. When we go through life being entitled to everything going only in our way, we can hardly expect to be happy and have to face challenges that are genuinely difficult. Here an important question arises: how do we practically apply Stoicism in life?

(6) Negative visualization: Negative visualization is one of the proposals put forth by Stoicism. It is an idea that we constantly visualize our fears rather than focusing on our goals. Instead of picturing things according to the plan, we visualize images at their very worst. Imagine what will happen if our plans keep on failing and what life would be like if all of our worst fears came true. Negative visualization first helps us to prepare for those worst case scenarios. Once we know what our fears actually look like, we can then think about how we would cope in that scenario. Often, we will find that this worst-case scenario is not as bad as we at first thought it would be. In other cases, we can actually find ways to cope up with such situations. This removes fears that could otherwise hold us back and means that we are not blindly ignoring what could potentially go wrong.

The general idea here is that we should not only visualize our worst case scenario, but also try living it. That might mean spending a week living with less money in hands or it might even mean sleeping in an uncomfortable environment. In either case, it teaches us not only that we can handle our worst fears and thus have less reason to be afraid, but also that we actually do not need material possessions in order to be content. Although cultivating such an approach is very important, it demands self-control and great discipline to part with our possessions and belongings. However, the result is freedom from fear and also from many physical restrictions. If we are weighed down by possessions and belongings, then we will not be able to move and progress freely. We will spend a lot of time on things that do not help us towards our determined goals. Ultimately, we will have much more to fear.

A person should realise that the more one owns, the more one has to lose. This results in a sense of insecurity and fear. Therefore, we should try to declutter and live a more focussed and minimalist life. Although it is challenging in modern times, at the very least, we should learn to detach ourselves from excessive physical possessions and remember that they are merely material things. They are a means to an end and if we must sacrifice them, so be it. Moreover, sacrificing our long awaited wish, for example turning down a desire to buy a smart watch in order to pay for your child's fees or parents' medicines are fine examples of warrior-like approach.

(7) Wear ordinary clothes as far as possible: Most people will disagree, but another classic enduring move is to wear ordinary clothes as much as possible in order to teach ourselves not to be ashamed, although we can afford. People might stare, comment and make fun, but this will simply teach that it does not matter at all what others think or talk about us. The only thing that matters is what we think about ourselves. This is an important aspect of the warrior mindset. Caring what other people think makes us vulnerable to peer pressure and narcissism. Occasionally, to do what must be done, a person must be willing to sacrifice his/her reputation for the righteous lifestyle.

(8) Expect the worst: Stoics argue that we use swear words when we are angry. Such anger is our own failure that is born from immaturity and foolishness. Recall about the last time you cursed in rage. Chances are that it was not because you were in debt or it rained. More likely, it was because you dropped something on your toe, or because you broke your much-loved possession. The point is that the anger comes from the surprise, not the disappointment. You do not swear when it rains because you know that rain is a likelihood. Thus, if you are angry, then it suggests that you did not anticipate whatever happened and this is possibly your own fault. If you accept that bad things happen and sometimes things do not go according to the plan, then you will have no need to be angry as you will be prepared mentally for it. Now, when your partner cheats on you, or when a service provider does not deliver a timely good service, you will think of it as being simply a part of life, just like the rain.

(9) Controlled reaction: Stoicism means submitting to the fact that you have barely any control over. At the same time, it also means taking solace in the knowledge that these outside factors can not hurt you, but only your reaction can. Sometimes we cannot control what happens to us, but can control what we make of that event and our own interpretation of it. Being mentally prepared for things that could go wrong is one good example. Similarly, though you might also simply decide not to let things affect you, to take a step back from them and to deal with the consequences rather than thrashing against things that we cannot change. Mindfulness and the ability to decide how we want to react to the things going on around us, we should remember that hard-hitting things happen. It is our job to deal with them and find our own way.

Rocky Balboa, one of the great modern Stoics quoted, "*Let me tell you something you already know. The world isn't all sunshine and rainbows. It's a very mean and nasty place and I don't care how tough you are, it will beat you to your knees and keep you there permanently if you let it. You, me, or nobody is gonna hit as hard as life. But isn't about how hard you hit, it's about how hard you can get hit, and keep moving forward. How much you can take, and keep moving forward. That's how winning is done.*"

(10) Cowards die many times before their deaths: It is true that if you live life in fear of death, then you will be permanently cautious. You will not take risks and as a result you will not live life to its fullest.

'Cowards die many times before their deaths', is a proverb written by English poet and playwright William Shakespeare. It explains to us that cowards die many times in their lives before they actually die. A coward lives in continuous fear. Only by thinking about his death, his heart and mind begins to shiver with fear. A coward believes that death is a huge hulk who is always hanging over him.

Every day we meet and face new challenges. It is our choice to accept or ignore them. Only brave people have the courage to head-on the challenges and go beyond boundaries. It is important to know that great discoveries, conquests and accomplishments happened only because courageous people decided to do it.

It is not a sign of courage to hide or run away from the troubles in life. A coward must understand that death is unavoidable. Natural disasters like tsunami, earthquakes, famines and floods make a coward shake with fear. He thinks that his death is near. He spends many sleepless nights. Moreover, due to wars, riots and other conflicts in society a coward further becomes a sacred-cat.

A coward sees everything in life with uncertainty and unpredictability. If some day he is standing at a bus stop, suddenly he feels that the bus will crash in the bus stop and kill him. Even while walking on the street he remains extra cautious. He walks from the extreme corner of the footpath. While crossing a road he is over careful to avoid an accident that may take his life. Imagining his death does not allow him to live happily and peacefully. If he receives the news of someone's death, he feels relieved for his escape from the death. Such is the outlook of a coward and hence, 'Cowards die many times before their deaths'.

Those who are not cowards accept death gracefully like warriors. They are aware that death is a natural event that has to occur some day or the other. Such people accept death with courage. Whether rich or poor, young or old, king or beggar, no one has overwhelmed death. However, untimely death is a heart-breaking reality. This can spread grief and terrify many people. As no one can challenge death, it is wise to adopt an accepting approach towards it rather than suffering the torturous imagination of death like a coward.

Coward people keep delaying their tasks and ignore their duties. A wise person with a strong mental approach would not do so. He wakes up, prepares himself and faces his fears with courage. Just as a chick comes out from an egg with a great force, our triumph comes only when we break ourselves free from fears. Only we can bring out the hidden bravery inside us at the frontage. Life comes once; we have to live it right.

CHAPTER FIVE

Mental Toughness

It is equally important to be willing for discomforts and experience small amounts of adversities. For instance, how can we lose weight if we are afraid of dieting? How can we expect to progress in our career if we do not have skills, dedication and avoid doing hard work? This is the reality for many of us. We are simply unwilling to do things we do not wish to do, or undergo hard times. We have become exceedingly weak and it is ultimately making us unhappy. Consider the difference between a dog and a wolf. A dog might be loving, loyal and fun, but it is entirely dependent on the master. It will not survive a day in the wild as it is certainly not a fighter like the wolf. The main reason is that the dog has been domesticated and made dependent.

This is the problem we as humans face. We have not only become domesticated by our comforts but have also become lazy, spoiled and overly indulged. In modern and fast moving society everything is disposable and everything comes easily with the help of money. Most of the time we run out of patience. Hungry? Visit a food outlet, order on phone or takeaway at home. The food will be packed with salt, sugar and/or different sauces making our cravings satisfied. Similarly, Bored? Turn on the television and laugh at something which is not so sensible.

Need information? Google it or just ask Alexa or Siri. Horny? Watch some porn. Want to get into better shape? No! That seems like climbing a steep mountain barefoot.

Being so constantly indulged in whatever we want means that we find it harder than ever to put in effort when it is needed. Why would we put in effort when we can have so much, so easily? When we are used to getting whatever we want with less effort, we start to take things for granted. For instance, we feel absolutely upset when the shower does not heat up properly. On the other hand, in the forest we would have only cold water to use. Eating would have required hunting or scavenging in the rain while avoiding predators. We could be so much stronger and tougher, mentally as well as physically. On the contrary, most of us are obese, lazy and low on motivation.

(1) Getting tough: We should try to live and feel satisfied with less. Travelling is an incredible way to help develop the warrior mindset. That means travelling and staying in inns or hotels without advance booking and only carrying a few clothes. One of my friends has been on a few solo trips like that. Once he went on a trip somewhere around North India, taking only a backpack. He narrated to me... Lying on a bench at a railway station in the snow, unable to read the signboards and not knowing when the next train would arrive. As it was before the internet's existence, taking its help was out of the question. Soon he discovered a little tea stall and managed to have some sweet steamy tea. He said he actually felt bliss drinking his tea from that white polystyrene cup. He appreciated the moment so much as it had been so long and he was feeling so cold. During his visits to me, he asks for his tea in a white polystyrene cup and thus, I have to store a few in the house. It travels him back to that blissful moment.

Sometimes we must carry our activities without certain comforts. We can discover those little things that can bring us a lot of joy. There is reward and happiness to be found in every moment. We do not need everything to go smoothly and perfectly. In fact, when things go wrong, it creates experiences and helps us to grow wiser and stronger.

(2) The growth of the mindset: Every challenge that crosses our path is an opportunity to get a tougher, smarter and improved version of our own self. By dealing with hardships, our life has greater purpose because life turns out to be meaningless when it is easy. We become better equipped to take on similar challenges in future. Therefore, the next time we find ourselves in debt, instead of letting it defeat us, we must see it as a challenge to be conquered. Taking care of health and focusing on earning more money to change the situation is always advisable. We should not stumble in stress and anxiety as it simply helps no one. See it as a chance to grow and prevent the same to happen again. Take the necessary steps and do not worry about how it looks to others. Do not keep blaming yourself for landing into that particular situation. Instead just take correct steps and learn from it. Say to yourself, "Although I was not good enough before, now I am going to be better."

Growth and challenges actually strengthen our brain. We thrive when we are challenged mentally and physically. It keeps us motivated and focussed, helping us to make correct decisions at the correct time. Not only should we welcome the challenges that cross our path, but also learn something new out of them. During peaceful times, we should prepare ourselves mentally, adopt necessary steps and skills as well as train our mind and body.

CHAPTER SIX

Challenging Self Towards Motivation

The initiative of having goal oriented behaviour is the result of motivation. The actual purpose of motivation is to decrease the mental or physical stress and increase the reasons of happiness in a person. Intrinsic and extrinsic are the two types of motivation. The intrinsic motivation is displayed through delight in a given situation. Such motivation is within the individual itself. On the other hand, extrinsic motivation is exhibited or enhanced by external factors such as money, reinforcements, gifts, pressure, etc.

If a person is strongly motivated to achieve or gain something huge in life, then that person is involved in aiming high for the future. This is the reason why motivation is intertwined with challenges. Moreover, we are physically and mentally designed in such a way that we are always ready to accept and face different challenges.

Motivation can be explained further by one of the following circumstances. If, for instance, one comes to know that he/she is in danger, then the immediate response would be to take all the necessary precautionary measures in order to prevent themselves from the danger to ensure safety. As such a situation challenges one's security and life, it manages to increase one's motivation towards the act of protecting themselves. In this manner, we need to engage ourselves in various challenges so that our confidence and impetus remain boosted. Facing and overcoming the challenges tends to impart a positive feeling that increases one's motivation. It also makes us test our patience and to what extent we can stretch ourselves.

The best way to deal and involve challenges in our lifestyle and daily routine is by setting goals and trying to accomplish them successfully. A person's general character and personality are formed through learning and practicing the standards and ethics of the social culture. As all the values do not have a positive influence on us, one must have a correct frame of mind full of motivation so that it becomes easy to create our own values and live accordingly. Constant reconditioning of the inner self would let a person see everything as a challenge and undergo the change of values that are needed. Too much relaxation of the brain would make a person feel like a lazy idler. Thus, it is healthier to keep the brain busy and in action.

It might be tiring to keep ourselves up to the challenges that life throws all the time, but when we become used to it, we can master the skills of being motivated and successful.

CHAPTER SEVEN

Developing Inner Self to Face Life Challenges

Everything begins from our mind. The smallest thought generated in mind changes into an idea, which takes the shape of an action in order to be applied. This whole process is functioned within one's mind to plan ahead. Hence, positivity is an important thinking approach that all successful people possess. We all have positivity inside us. It is only a matter of choice for us to use it or not. People who are positive in their approaches attract us more than those who are negative and always blame others or their environment for their failures.

Our thought processes are controlled by our mind. These processes are reflected and exhibited by our behaviour, attitude and insight. It also shows the type of lifestyle we would prefer. Those who are happy tend to have positive thinking which emits around them. However, those who are gloomy have a negative aura that emits around them. Hence, it is up to us as to what type of lifestyle we prefer, positive or negative.

Happiness and misery, both are important elements of life. No matter how wealthy one is, one can certainly never avoid neither happiness nor misery. These problems which encircle us tend to make us stronger internally as they teach us about life, about values and how to face different challenges that we come across in our daily life. It is generally seen that those who face challenges positively have positive outcomes. On the other hand, those who face challenges with a negative attitude, usually end up with negative results.

- **Following are some of the important guidelines which helps us to improve our daily routine and develop a stronger inner self:**

(a) While facing negative thoughts and trying to change them into positive ones, we can control our thoughts and thoughts should not be controlling the way we live.

(b) Instead of complaining and accusing others around us, we should accurately assess our options. Think of the best possible solution under the given circumstances and act accordingly upon them.

(c) Avoid being around negative people. Stay in the company of those who think positively. Talk and get consultation from people who tend to behave and think confidently and firmly. They are a source of inspiration.

(d) Find happiness in simple things in life. Remember to look upon the less fortunate and deprived people and be grateful for what you already have.

(e) Love yourself instead of blaming, as it never helps. Be kind and respectful to others. Express small gestures of kindness such as a simple smile and hello to people around. The positive signals we send out are met with positivity in response. This increases our satisfaction levels.

(f) Help the unfortunate and needy ones by giving them voluntary service. Spend time with the people living in misery and release your positivity onto them. However, such services are performed on one's own free will.

To conclude we can say that we get what we give. We must send indications of positivity and give hope to others. When we give others a reason to smile for and hope to cherish, we will get the same in return.

CHAPTER EIGHT

Exercise and Strength

By now we already know that the warrior mindset involves greater discipline, resilience, patience, calmness and strength. However, the real question is how we get to that point to gain such a mindset? Hopefully by now we have understood what the warrior mindset is all about and what it means in a broader context. However, how can we overcome our weaknesses or an urge to eat unhealthy or to always relax and select the easy options?

- **Following are a few powerful tools that will help us to grow and become stronger:**

(1) Meditation: Meditation is an absolute must for a modern warrior to regain composure. This is one of the single most influential tools for transforming the mindset. It provides the elasticity, self-assurance and sense of calmness one needs to choose while reacting through various emotions and feelings. Meditation is simply the practice of concentrating the mind by emptying the brain from the thoughts which in turn helps in learning to avoid distracting ideas and instincts. However, this demands great mental discipline.

Meditation further teaches us to not be distracted from our anxieties, urges and desires. It helps in letting our thoughts drift by without affecting us, while transcendental experience (*going beyond human knowledge, experience or reason, especially in a religious or spiritual way*) clears our mind entirely. This is a great way to calm our physiology when stressed or aroused and to take back control over our thoughts and actions. Those who meditate are calmer and less easily provoked as it frees them to act in the most considered and effective manner.

In simple words, meditation is a great way to recharge our batteries and gain more energy. This in turn allows us to execute our plans in a proper fashion. One of my author friends once mentioned that he wakes up at five in the morning while his wife and daughters are still asleep. He meditates before they get up. How does it feel? According to him, although it does not feel like anything special, there is surely some difference. At around one in the afternoon like before his head does not hit the decks. Without practicing meditation daily, by one his head gets heavy and sleepy like most of the people. He succeeds in gliding through the day and then again he meditates at around seven after reaching home.

(2) Correct breathing: Another tool we can use to regain our tranquillity and enter the warrior mindset is the correct pattern of breathing. This means belly breathing that includes breathing from our diaphragm first and taking deep breaths. This calms our nervous system and puts us into a resting state. It is the perfect way to overcome anxiety. Proper breathing starts in the nose and then moves to the stomach as our diaphragm contracts. The belly expands and our lungs are filled with air. It is the most efficient way to breathe, as it pulls down on the lungs. Thus, it creates negative pressure in the chest, resulting in air flowing into the lungs.

(3) Cold showers: Cold showers increase metabolism and help us produce more testosterone, causing a flood or adrenaline. (*Testosterone is a hormone, the chemical substances produced in the body that causes men to develop sexual and physical features that are characteristics of the male body. Adrenaline is a substance produced in the body when a person is angry, excited or afraid. It makes the heart beat faster and increases our energy and ability to move quickly).* They also strengthen the immune system. In other words, they are good for us and a great way to start the day. Although such practice is a terrible shock to the system, precisely it is ideal for the training of a stronger mind. Taking cold showers requires incredible mental discipline and if we can force ourselves to do this every day, then we can achieve just about anything.

(4) Walking: Walking is one of the most effective and natural exercises known by man. It is believed that our two legs are our personal doctors. These doctors are used by a person for walking and running to stay fit. Walking is slower than running. The speeds of walking vary depending on the factors like height, weight, age, efforts, surface and fitness of the individual. Walking is a great way to get in shape. It is simple to do, mild in its influence and does not require any equipment or gym space. A person can follow his/her walking schedule on a treadmill or outdoors to reach a particular goal.

While walking is a natural body movement, it is a great exercise for obese people. Walking is one of the easiest and cheapest ways to keep oneself fit. Experts have approved that prolonged walking sessions for a period of thirty minutes to an hour a day shows benefits on the human body. Any exercise can burn calories but brisk walking helps in burning the stored fats. It is effective for burning internal belly fat, which not only contributes to the waistline, but also increases the risk for diabetes, high blood pressure and heart problems. Brisk walking is also considered as a great cardio exercise, helping in toning the legs and reducing the thigh fat. Among several health benefits of walking, some of them are reducing the risk of high blood pressure, cancer, depression, obesity, diabetes, etc. It also helps the person to sleep well, upsurges the health of the bones, strengthens the hipbone and most importantly increases life expectancy.

Specialists agree that regular physical activity is one of the basis for good health and walking is one of the stress-free physical activities. All one needs is a pair of comfortable shoes and walking can be done almost anywhere and at any time. Walking as a form of exercise can also be done by aged people.

Since ages, walking has been the most natural exercise known to man. Besides this, there are other miraculous benefits of walking. It improves blood circulation. Calf muscles are said to be man's extra heart. While walking, these muscles pump the blood to the heart with all force, minimizing the dangers of heart attack. Walking also decreases fatigue. Moreover, lower backache, which is a common complaint, gradually disappears. Above all, the body gains its proper shape, improves posture and reduces anxiety and overall stiffness. Importantly it also improves one's temper.

(5) Strength training and significance of physical activities: Once Greek philosopher Socrates said, "*No man has the right to be an amateur in the matter of physical training. It is a shame for a man to grow old without seeing the* *beauty and strength of which his body is capable*." What do all the warriors through history have in common? They are not just mentally tough, (although that has been the focus of this book), they are also physically tough. This is very important because physical toughness gives us the strength, the resolve and the power to be confident and to make a stand when we do need to fight for our values. One should avoid fights, but actually being formidable physically helps an individual to avoid the need to fight. Moreover, it gives an ability to protect the ones we love.

We know that our body is made of muscles, blood, bones, flesh, organs and more than two hundred types of cells that can all be classified into various tissues. When any of these things are injured or do not function well, our body suffers. Nobody likes to be in pain or fall ill. Therefore, it is important that we keep our body healthy and fit by exercising regularly. Physical activity or exercise can be defined as, 'any bodily movement produced by skeletal muscles that requires energy.' Thus, physical activity includes all activities or exercises performed during the day.

Exercising is one of the most important ways of keeping our body healthy. If we do not exercise, over a period of time, our muscles become weak and we find difficulties in carrying out our day-to-day activities. In addition, the bones can become weak leading to frequent injuries. Regular physical activity can improve our health and minimises the risk of developing several life threatening diseases. Exercise can have immediate and long-term health benefits. Most importantly, regular activity can improve our overall quality of life.

Some of the most important benefits of regular exercise are maintaining body weight, helping in enhancing memory, the sleep quality improves, lowers the risks of chronic diseases, increases our energy levels, increases self-esteem and self-confidence, makes us feel happy all day and strengthens muscles and bones. Exercise is a scientifically proven mood booster and decreases the symptoms of both depression and anxiety.

A person can perform several exercises, including playing a sport. Walking, jogging, swimming, running, cycling, tracking, etc. improves cardio. Aged people prefer using less physical and/or mental energy. For fitter one's, there are rock-climbing, aerobics and other physically challenging activities. Regular physical activity can improve our muscle strength and enhance our endurance levels. Exercise delivers oxygen and nutrients to our tissues and helps the cardiovascular system to work more efficiently. With the improved health of heart and lung, a warrior has more energy to go on with his/her daily tasks.

People exercise to keep their body healthy, but some end up injuring themselves badly. Physical activities and exercises release chemicals in the brain that improve one's mood. It makes us feel stress-free and reduces depression. It even enhances our morale and self-esteem. Therefore, regular physical activities and exercises have a great impact in the life of a warrior.

CHAPTER NINE

Being Yourself as a Warrior

There is no example of a nation benefiting from prolonged warfare. In other words, if we are at odds with a competitor or a colleague then a prolonged struggle will only serve to damage the both. This is called a 'pyrrhic victory'. It is a phrase that comes from some famous historical battle. By the end even if we win, we would have damaged our reputation and wasted resources. Thus, even after winning, we are left with nothing, but a pyrrhic victory. The best option is to turn an opponent into an ally and find a way that both can benefit from.

A warrior chooses his battles wisely. His mindset is not about being aggressive and conservative but about being poised, forgiving and powerful enough to not need to lift a finger. A famous quote suggests, "*The supreme art of war is to subdue the enemy without fighting.*" This is more relevant to modern warriors than ever before.

Constant success changes one's conduct with time. This is particularly important to note if a person runs a large successful organization and abruptly is in danger of resting on his achievements. Thinking one step ahead at all times is necessary to avoid a sudden bad fate. This repeats the views we discussed earlier about being willing to change the principles and adapt where necessary. However, this should come from within and not forcefully.

Crushing the opponents and employees may not be encouraged in ethical business. At the same time, do not make enemies and give them time to lick their wounds to once again stand up and attack. As far as possible, the warrior should avoid combat and confrontation. He should seek to please everyone and find the most mutually beneficial outcome. However, if he decides to engage in competition or combat, then he must act with conclusiveness. The wise man does at once what the fool does finally. Time is money and indecisiveness is a perfect recipe for failure. Entrepreneurs are simply those who understand that there is little difference between obstacle and opportunity and are able to turn both to their advantage. Opening a fish tin can be a challenge or an opportunity. This is similar to the ideas we discussed earlier about seeing challenges as a chance for growth and development. The warrior mindset is timeless. It is just as important today as it was ever before as anything can approach a warrior.

(1) Being yourself: We all need to learn to be our very own selves. This is one of the most crucial aspects to successfully navigate through the life challenges. Healing ourselves from the hurts and pains caused by others requires hard work and constant efforts to get rid of our negative traits.

Traits such as arrogance, rudeness, dishonesty and stinginess should not have any place in life. When we proudly walk around with these ugly habits, we are inviting all sorts of negativity into our lives. This results in more pain and disappointment. Hence, it is always desirable to know your own self. This will better prepare you to heal by learning more about your own flaws.

For being yourself we have to distance ourselves from all the labels imposed by the environment around us. These ugly labels can be the way we look, dress, speak or even the community in which we grew and belong. There remains no reason for us to let others squeeze us into a thing that does not really respect or represent us. Imagine how liberating it would be not to pretend to be someone we are not. We would never want to take certain liberties for granted that may have far-reaching effects on our personal life and may even threaten our jobs or relations.

- **Following are some of the important reasons why we need to start being true to self:**

(a) You will never be able to please everyone. If you constantly allow the people around you to determine who you are, you will have to change what you stand for in order to try and make them happy. The only problem with this is that you will be dealing with so many conflicting demands that you will eventually end up disappointing someone. Additionally, putting yourself under this kind of pressure will leave you feeling dissatisfied in the end.

(b) Several times society around us fails to understand what it actually wants. The media portrays both the humbled homemaker and the fierce achiever as an ideal woman. Similarly, society demands man to be sensitive towards the needs of others as well as firm in decision making. Which will you be if you are simply allowing those around you to determine who you actually are? Whatever you decide to be, it is important to know that every day it is quite exhausting to be the kind of person you are not.

(c) You will end up making life-changing decisions based on the urges of the people around you, who will not suffer the consequences of your choices. For example: If you decide to have a child, simply because your family thinks it is time, you will be the one to take care of that child. If you decide to pursue a particular career because your parents or peers think you would do well in it, you will have to live with the burden of a wrong career that you never liked in the first place.

(d) Sooner or later the truth always comes out. People will begin to realize that you are faking. Unfortunately, as we see in the case of many celebrities, the truth often comes out in a big scandal or collapse.

(e) When you are gratified with who you are, you will emerge as a true life warrior. You can never be happy or love yourself when you are constantly pretending to be someone you are actually not.

(f) When all is said and done, you need to take total control of your life if you want to see a newer version of self. You cannot expect different results if you are not bold enough to make drastic and different changes. The real time for those changes is now.

CHAPTER TEN

Conclusion

Together we have reached towards the end of our book's journey. However, your journey has just begun, as it is time to start putting yourself out there, testing yourself, growing, emerging, taking on different challenges and deciding what is most important to you. It is time to stop upsetting yourself with the small issues, to indulge into creature comforts and to embrace a more exciting and demanding life. This will help in discovering the real value of life and that is what will make you great as an individual.

As a word of caution, this is not going to be as easy as you expect. Sometimes you are going to find that doing the right thing and ignoring your emotional response means saying things that people hate the most.

About The Author

FIROZ TATA (Wolfy) is a non-practicing priest, an author, a poet, notion creator, a storyteller and a national level cyclist from Mumbai, India. He is credited to win several prestigious medals and trophies in the sport of cycling. He has been fascinating and increasing his circle of nationwide readers with his academic as well as fictional writings for nearly 15 years.

He has shown his strong writing influence through informative and imaginative essays, instructive letters, heart-warming poems, engrossing stories and captivating quotes depicting resolve, love, women, beauty, life and hopes. However, he is a single man, perhaps patiently waiting for someone. He firmly believes to love and to be loved loyally and passionately from a distance rather than sticking in an intolerable and suffocative relationship.

Due to his deserted, suppressive and cut off childhood and adolescent years from the outer world, he had no other alternative but to develop a deep passion and skills for writing since his early days. Back then, as a child, he was destined to encounter numerous terrible experiences with his several teachers. He also had his share of horrible experiences at home that no child deserves.

After failing miserably in English in the last and decisive year of his schooling, no one but only him through the burning desire, dedication and determination in his heart knew that one day he would become a published author. Years later, he successfully did. Even today, he is dedicated to the path of enriching himself with knowledge and improving with the passing years.

By now, he has authored nearly 60 academic as well as fictional books for various publishers. His works also include nearly 500 essays and 800 quotes in his total 16 creative writing books. All his books are strongly recommended not only for the bookshelves of children, but also adults. His works are highly appreciated and acclaimed by several readers, educationalists and publishers.

Some Other Books By Firoz Tata

Augmenting Your Knowledge
My Comprehension Hub
The Gist of Informal Letter Writing
The Gist of Formal Letter Writing
The Glorious History of Ancient India
The Glorious Landmarks in World History
Maa Saraswati Subodh Hindi Grammar
Maa Saraswati 600 Muhavare aur Kahawate
Clustering Rhymes
Fragrance
My Purple Lotus
Woohoo! It's a Tale Time
Great Stories of Mama and Delzin
A Door to Short Stories
Paving Your Success
Paving Your Path Towards Self-healing
Womb of the Universe
Conquering Insomnia
Flying Colours
The Connecting Hearts
16 June
Forehead Forever
Purple

These and many other books written by Firoz Tata (Wolfy) are available on the publisher's site notionpress.com (With read instant feature), on national and international Amazon sites in paperback and Kindle formats and also on flipkart.com

Kindly share your valuable reviews and suggestions on reviewmypublications@gmail.com

Those readers interested in joining Wolfy Books WhatsApp group, kindly send an email on the above given email address.

9 798888 151358

Printed by Libri Plureos GmbH in Hamburg,
Germany